W9-CDY-684

Be a Friend

MY FIRST MANNERS

Written by Constance Allen and Elizabeth Clasing
Illustrated by Joel Schick

Published by Phoenix International Publications, Inc.
8501 West Higgins Road, Suite 300, Chicago, Illinois 60631
Lower Ground Floor, 59 Gloucester Place, London W1U 8JJ

www.pikidsmedia.com

p i kids is a trademark of Phoenix International Publications, Inc., and is registered in the United States.

8 7 6 5 4 3 2 1

ISBN: 978-1-4127-6784-2

phoenix international publications, inc.

Hello, there! It is I, your furry pal Grover,
here to tell you: There is nothing like
a little niceness from a friend
when you are trying new things.

I can remember the first time
I tried to ride a bicycle.

It was not easy. And I felt a
teensy little bit afraid.

Thanks to many kind words,
I was not afraid to try anymore.
And look what I can do now!

Even the very bravest monster needs
a friendly cheer now and then.

... or even the second time ...

I believe you are getting better at this!

But take it from your friend Grover.
Just keep those kind words coming.

With a little encouragement, an adorable
monster can succeed at anything!